Step By Step to Stand-Up Comedy

Workbook 2:
How to Improve Jokes and Routines

By Greg Dean

Cover by Kurt Reichenbach

ISBN: 978-0-9897351-1-7

Dedication

To my amazing wife, Gayla Johnson-Dean,
whose never ending love and dedication
saw me through my cancer to a complete cure.

Table of Contents

Introduction

In Greg Dean's *Step By Step to Stand-Up Comedy – Workbook Series, Workbook 2: How to Improve Jokes and Routines* you'll learn techniques to improve your jokes and then how to assemble them into a performable routine. This workbook covers Chapter 3 and Chapter 4 of my paperback, eBook, or audio book of *Step By Step to Stand-Up Comedy*.

Suggestions and Requirements
To complete all the exercises effectively, there are several things you'll need to do:

• Have At Least Twenty Jokes
Once you have several jokes you can begin to polish and arrange them into a routine. If you've done *Workbook 1: How to Write Jokes*, then you should have enough jokes to use in this workbook. If you have not read *Workbook 1: How to Write Jokes*, then I suggest you get it and learn the joke writing mechanisms along with the *Joke Prospector*, our innovative joke writing system. If you're already performing and have material you want to improve, and then by all means use those jokes in the exercises.

• Pick One Location to Do Your Joke Writing and Writing Exercises
As part of Greg Dean's overall method to learn to be funny, Dean asks you to separate your critical and creative skills so they're done in different locations and at different times. For this section, pick one location where you'll do all your analytical joke writing and writing exercises. Later, in *Workbook 3: How to Remember Jokes Naturally*, you'll select a separation location to practice all of your rehearsal and performing exercises to eliminate self-criticism from your rehearsal and therefore your performance.

• Place Post-Its on the Answers to Exercises Pages
To make it easy for you to turn from an exercise to the answers, place Post-Its on pages 53 – 57 with the page number written on it. You'll be glad you did.

* * *

With the twenty or more jokes and your locations selected to do your writing, you're now ready to improve and routine your material. By completing all the exercises in this workbook, you'll have your material ready for a great comedy show.

From Funny to Funnier

In this section you'll learn some basic guidelines for sharpening your jokes as well as a few techniques for expanding on them. These methods come from my own experience as a working comic as well as from the tried and true writing techniques of successful comedians I've worked with over the years.

ECONOMY

Nothing kills a good joke more certainly than smothering it with an avalanche of unnecessary words and information. Both setups and punches should be short and concise. Take your longer jokes and edit out all the unnecessary words.

It's Your Turn!

On the form below, rewrite the sample to make it shorter.

Joke: *"Postal workers put in hours of overtime. They leave the post office*

and go to a bar and drink for hours."

Rewrite: _____

_____

Answer on page 53

Next, find some of your jokes that are over written. Write them on the forms below and on page 3 and then rewrite them by removing all the unnecessary words.

Note: it is possible to edit to the point where the joke no longer makes sense. Read the joke aloud to someone else to make sure the setup and punch still communicates the idea of the joke.

Joke: _____

_____

Rewrite: _____

_____

Joke: _____

_____

Rewrite: _____

_____

Joke: _____

_____

Rewrite: _____

_____

Joke: _____

_____

Rewrite: _____

_____

Joke: _____

_____

Rewrite: _____

_____

END THE PUNCH WITH THE REVEAL

In every joke there's a pivotal word, phrase, or action which reveals the reinterpretation which I call the *reveal*. To effectively write a joke, make sure your reveal appears as close as possible to the *end* of the punch.

Here are the two ways a reveal is incorrectly placed in a joke:

• Unnecessary words are said or actions are done after the reveal

Talking past the reveal is one of the most common and irritating errors. It usually occurs because the comic inserts mindless prattle beyond the point where the joke pops a laugh.

Identify the jokes where you talk past the reveal and rewrite it so the reveal is at the end.

It's Your Turn!

Rewrite the sample jokes by removing the useless information to place the reveal at the end of the punch.

Joke: *"He has a contagious smile. Chlamydia or some other disgusting*

oral disease."

Rewrite: _____

_____

Answer on page 53

Next, go through all of your jokes and identify the reveals. Write those jokes on the forms below and on page 5 that have extraneous babble written past the reveals. Then rewrite your jokes to place the reveals as close to the end of the punches as possible.

Joke: _____

_____

Rewrite: _____

_____

Joke: _____

_____

Rewrite: _____

_____

Joke: _____

_____

Rewrite: _____

_____

Joke: _____

_____

Rewrite: _____

_____

Joke: _____

_____

Rewrite: _____

_____

Joke: _____

_____

Rewrite: _____

_____

• The reveal gets mixed up with other important information
It's imperative to identify the reveal. Otherwise it may get mixed up with less important information needed to make the joke work.

It's Your Turn!

Rewrite the sample joke below by placing the reveal to the end of the punch.

Joke: *"After just four karate lessons, I could use my cast to break a two* ___

inch board." ___

Rewrite: ___

___

Answer on page 53

Next, comb through your jokes find the ones that may have two important words or phrases in the punch. Write those jokes on the forms below and on page 7.

Then rewrite the jokes by reversing the words or phrases to put the reveal at the end of the punches.

Joke: ___

___

Rewrite: ___

___

Joke: _____

_____

Rewrite: _____

_____

Joke: _____

_____

Rewrite: _____

_____

Joke: _____

_____

Rewrite: _____

_____

Joke: _____

_____

Rewrite: _____

_____

USE WORDS OR PHRASES WITH HARD CONSONANTS

The hard consonant sounds, especially "K" sounds which include hard "C" and "Qu" and, to a lesser extent, "T", "P", hard "G", "D" and "B," tend to make words sound funnier. Using words with these hard consonants instead of synonyms with softer sounds really helps improve a joke.

It's Your Turn!

Using the sample joke below, rewrite it by selection had consonant words to replace the marked words.

Joke: *"I hate singles bars. Guys come up to me and say, 'Hey, sweetie,*

can I buy you a drink?' I say, 'No, but I'll take the three dollars.'"

Rewrite: _____

_____

Answer on page 54

Next, look through all your material to find jokes that might be improved by replacing soft consonant words with hard consonant words. Write the jokes on the forms below or on page 9.

Then rewrite the jokes that have soft consonant words with synonyms that have hard consonants.

Joke: _____

_____

Rewrite: _____

_____

Joke: _____

_____

Rewrite: _____

_____

Joke: _____

_____

Rewrite: _____

_____

Joke: _____

_____

Rewrite: _____

_____

Joke: _____

_____

Rewrite: _____

_____

USE RHYTHMS OF THREE

Here's how rhythms of three jokes work: the setup presents two items to create a pattern, hence the target assumption. Then the punch gives the third item that breaks the pattern, with a reinterpretation that is unexpected, yet still compatible with the first two items. The jokes that can be improved with a rhythm of three are the ones that have lists with no comedic payoff.

It's Your Turn!

The sample joke below contains a list that doesn't end with a joke. Rewrite the list into a rhythm of three joke. You're searching for a third item that fits the pattern of the first two items on the list, but is still completely unexpected.

Joke with List: *"I can persuade any woman to sleep with me just with* _____

flowers, chocolates, and some romantic music." _____

Rhythm of Three: _____

_____

Answer on page 54

Next, search through your material to find jokes that contain lists that don't end with an unexpected item and write them on the forms below or on page 11.

Then rewrite each list into a rhythm of three where the first two items create a pattern, and the third item breaks the pattern, but is still compatible with the first two.

Joke with List: _____

_____

Rhythm of Three: _____

_____

Joke with List: _____

_____

Rhythm of Three: _____

_____

Joke with List: _____

_____

Rhythm of Three: _____

_____

Joke with List: _____

_____

Rhythm of Three: _____

_____

Joke with List: _____

_____

Rhythm of Three: _____

_____

STICK TO THE COMMON REALM OF KNOWLEDGE

If they don't understand what you're talking about, they won't laugh. When a certain word or reference is crucial to the understanding of a joke, you must consider whether it's familiar to your audience. Sometimes you'll need to use a more familiar alternative.

It's Your Turn!

Using the sample joke below, replace the marked person with a more modern reference.

Joke: *"I think* Vlad the Impailer *would have enjoyed watching the* _____

Three Stooges." _____

Rewrite: _____

_____

Answer on page 54

Next, comb through your jokes to find the ones with references that require inside knowledge or are not in common use and write them on the forms below.

Then rewrite your jokes with common language everyone can understand.

Joke: _____

_____

Rewrite: _____

_____

Joke: _____

_____

Rewrite: _____

_____

WRITE DIALOGUE WHENEVER POSSIBLE

Many jokes are written from a narrative POV and describe the performer and the other people and their dialogue. Instead, identify your role and the characters' roles in the scene of the joke, and then write out the dialogue for yourself and the characters. This allows the performer to act out the scene of the joke as if it's happening in the present.

It's Your Turn!

Using the sample joke below, rewrite it by identifying the narrator, you in the scene, and the character. Then write it out with the appropriate dialogue.

Narrator Joke: *"Recently, I was driving and my car got rear ended. My* _____

friend Bob ask me if I was alright. I told him I couldn't tell until I talk to my _____

lawyer." _____

Dialogue: _____

_____

_____

Answer on page 55

Next, sift through your jokes to find the ones written entirely as the narrator and write them on the forms below and on page 14.

Then rewrite each joke by starting with the narrator voice to set up the scene and then write out the dialogue for you and the character or between characters.

Narrator Joke: _____

_____

Dialogue: _____

_____

_____

Narrator Joke: _____

_____

Dialogue: _____

_____

_____

Narrator Joke: _____

_____

Dialogue: _____

_____

_____

Narrator Joke: _____

_____

Dialogue: _____

_____

_____

Narrator Joke: _____

_____

Dialogue: _____

_____

_____

MAKE YOUR CHARACTERS SPECIFIC AND REAL

One of the central differences between amateurs and pros is the depth of their characters. Making the characters in your jokes real and specific people greatly enhances the jokes' effectiveness.

Here's an example form for the joke and the character profile:

Joke: *"My mind is as sharp as it's ever been. Knock on wood."* **(Knocks on a wooden table, then looks at the door and yells.)** *"Come in."*

Name: Millard

Job: retired

Sex: male

Age: 86

Height: 5' 6"

Weight: 145

National Heritage: White

Voice: gravely and too loud

Posture: stooped over

Walk: slow and with a cane

Characteristics or Taints: hard of hearing and grumpy

General Attitude: self-righteous

Idiosyncrasies: scowls

Agenda: trying to prove he's not old.

Religion: not relevant

Once you know the general information about the character, now it's time to bring him or her to life. Become the character and do some activity, like cleaning your bathroom, washing the dishes or even going shopping. The idea is to spend time being the characters to understand how they think and behave differently than you.

Take notes on any revelations about the character.

Notes: He's grumpy and impatient. He's unaware that he talks too loud because he's hard of hearing. He gestures from the elbow and likes to point his finger at whoever he's talking to. He's senile and will have the same conversation again and again. If necessary, he will use his cane to hit if someone disagrees with him. If he loves you, he'll give you anything.

Rewrite the Joke: "Let me tell you youngins, my mind is as sharp as it ever been. Knock on wood." (Knocks on a wooden table, then looks at the door and yells.) "Come in."

It's Your Turn!

Search through your jokes for all the unexpressed characters. Select 2 jokes and write them on the forms located on page 17 and 19.

Then fill out the character profile form for each of your characters to create real and specific people.

CHARACTER PROFILE FORM #1

Joke: _____

_____

_____

Name: _____

Job: _____

Sex: _____

Age: _____

Height: _____

Weight: _____

National Heritage: _____

Voice: _____

Posture: _____

Walk: _____

Characteristics or Taints: _____

General Attitude: _____

Idiosyncrasies: _____

Agenda: _____

Religion: _____

Continue Your Turn!

Spend five minutes a day being each of your characters to bring them to life as real people. Get to know how he or she moves and speaks. If the character behaves just like you, then you don't have a character.

Take notes about what you've learn. Then rewrite the joke or bit to include the characters' new dialogue. The characters should have their own perspective on the situation, which should be very different from your own.

Notes after Being the Character: _____

_____

_____

_____

_____

Rewrite the Joke: _____

_____

_____

_____

CHARACTER PROFILE FORM #2

Joke: _____

_____

_____

Name: _____

Job: _____

Sex: _____

Age: _____

Height: _____

Weight: _____

National Heritage: _____

Voice: _____

Posture: _____

Walk: _____

Characteristics or Taints: _____

General Attitude: _____

Idiosyncrasies: _____

Agenda: _____

Religion: _____

Notes after Being the Character:

_____

_____

_____

_____

Rewrite the Joke:

_____

_____

_____

REGIONALIZE YOUR REFERENCES

Insert into your jokes the names of local landmarks, neighboring cities, regional hotels, stores, bars and restaurants to localize them for your current audience.

It's Your Turn!

Using the sample joke below, rewrite it and replace the marked generic term with a local reference.

Joke: *"Postal workers put in hours of overtime... at the bar."* _____

Regionalize: _____

Answer on page 55

Go through your jokes and search for the ones with landmark, store, school, hotel, bar or restaurant references and write them on the forms below or on page 22.

Circle the current references, and then rewrite the jokes using alternative regional references.

Joke: _____

_____

Regionalize: _____

_____

Joke: _____

_____

Regionalize: _____

_____

Joke: _____

_____

Regionalize: _____

_____

Joke: _____

_____

Regionalize: _____

_____

Joke: _____

_____

Regionalize: _____

_____

Joke: _____

_____

Regionalize: _____

_____

CALENDAR DAY JOKES

Have some jokes and routines for all of the special calendar dates such as Christmas, Halloween, Secretary's Day, Black History Month, etc. You can use these jokes year after year as each specific day comes around.

Here's an example:

Calendar Date: Valentine's Day

Joke or Bit: *"All my girlfriend wanted for Valentine's Day was a card.*

American Express Platinum."

It's Your Turn!

On the forms below and on page 24, pick some celebrated calendar days and then write a joke for each.

Calendar Day:

Joke or Bit:

Calendar Day:

Joke or Bit:

Calendar Day:

Joke or Bit:

Calendar Day: _____

Joke or Bit: _____

_____

Calendar Day: _____

Joke or Bit: _____

_____

Calendar Day: _____

Joke or Bit: _____

_____

Calendar Day: _____

Joke or Bit: _____

_____

USING GRAMMATICALLY INCORRECT LANGUAGE IS OKAY

People don't talk like they write, so you should write like they talk. Proper grammar and syntax have nothing to do with making a joke funny. In fact, stiffly worded jokes seldom flow as well as jokes written with the flaws and rhythms of everyday speech.

It's Your Turn!

Using the sample joke below, rewrite it to reflect the regional dialect implied by the character within the joke.

Formal Language: *"A guy from the Louisiana swamp told me they have mosquitoes so large that they have ticks."*

Common Language: _____

_____

Answer on page 55

Read through your jokes to find the ones written like formal literature and write them on the forms below and on page 26.

Read your jokes out loud so you can hear the places that are stiffly worded or contain unrealistic, flowery descriptions. Rewrite the jokes to mimic how your really speak. If you don't know how you really sound, then record yourself and copy your vocal quirks. For characters, find someone who speaks like that person or thing, and then copy that speech pattern. Then rewrite your jokes as you or the characters would really speak.

Formal Language: _____

_____

Common Language: _____

_____

Formal Language: _____

_____

Common Language: _____

_____

Formal Language: _____

_____

Common Language: _____

_____

Formal Language: _____

_____

Common Language: _____

_____

Formal Language: _____

_____

Common Language: _____

_____

FEEL FREE TO MAKE UP WORDS

Comedians get to create or change words to write jokes. The trick is to change the normal words, but still allow the audience to follow the joke with the made up word. There needs to be a connecting concept as with the example below. "Gyn" and "groin" sound similar and both deal with the concept of the crotch.

Normal: *"My wife has to go to the gynocogist."*

Made Up: *"My wife has to go see her groinocolgist."*

It's Your Turn!

Go through your jokes and search for normal words or word fragments that sound similar to other words or fragments. Write these jokes on the forms below and on page 28.

Next, decide on the similar sounding words or fragments you want to use to replace the normal words or fragments. Then replace the normal word or fragment with the similar sounding word or fragment to make up new words.

Normal: _____

_____

Made Up: _____

_____

Normal: _____

_____

Made Up: _____

_____

Normal: _____

_____

Made Up: _____

_____

Normal: _____

_____

Made Up: _____

_____

Normal: _____

_____

Made Up: _____

_____

SOMETIMES A SIGHT GAG IS BETTER

Sometimes seeing it is funnier than hearing it. There are many ways to do sight gags like hand gestures, signs, t-shirts, pantomimes, etc.

It's Your Turn!

Using the sample joke below, write a site gag for the punch.

Verbal Joke: *"All my girlfriend wanted for Valentine's Day was a card ...*

American Express Platinum."

Sight Gag: _____

_____

Answer on page 56

Sort through your jokes for punches that might be better communicated as a sight gag, and then write those jokes on the forms below or on page 30.

Then describe the sight gags that can replace your verbal punches.

Verbal Joke: _____

_____

Sight Gag: _____

_____

Verbal Joke: _____

_____

Sight Gag: _____

_____

Verbal Joke: _____

_____

Sight Gag: _____

_____

Verbal Joke: _____

_____

Sight Gag: _____

_____

Verbal Joke: _____

_____

Sight Gag: _____

_____

TAG YOUR JOKES

Tagging a joke is comic's slang for adding another punch to a completed joke. Getting two or more laughs from the initial setup is the most powerful technique for improving jokes and routines. Take the time to understand and practice the **three techniques** for tagging jokes.

Refer to **Workbook 1: How to Write Jokes** in the sections **The Secrets of Joke Structure** and the **Joke Mine** to thoroughly understand the terms target assumption, connector and reinterpretation used in this section.

Recap of Joke Mechanisms

At the center of all jokes is a **(C) connector,** which is one thing that has at least two meanings. The setup establishes a **(TA) target assumption**, which is the **expected** meaning of the connector. Then, the punch reveals a **(R) reinterpretation,** which is the **unexpected** meaning of the C - connector. The R - reinterpretation makes the TA - target assumption wrong, which completes the joke.

• Technique 1: Tag the Same Target Assumption and Connector, Again

It's Your Turn!

Using the sample jokes below and on page 32, first notice the setup's TA - target assumption, C - connector, and R - reinterpretation in parentheses.

Next, for the same C - connector, find a different meaning to create a new R - reinterpretation.

Then based on the new R - reinterpretation and considering the content of the punch, write a tag that also makes the TA- target assumption wrong, again.

Setup: *"For Father's Day I took my father out."*   TA - (to dinner)

C - (took out)

Punch: *"With a pair of scissors."*   R - (killed)

Same C - (took out)

Tag: _____ New R - (_____)

Answer on page 56

Setup: *"I play in a three piece band."*	TA - (three musicians)
	C - (three piece)
Punch: *"We wear a three piece suit."*	R - (suit with three pieces)
	Same C - (three piece)
Tag: _____	New R - (_____)

Answer on page 56

Continue Your Turn!

Using the forms below, write the setups and punches of your own one-liner jokes.

Next, fill in the parentheses with your TA - target assumption, C - connector, and R - reinterpretation.

Then based on the same TA - target assumption and C - connector, write a tag that shatters the original TA and C, again.

Setup: _____	TA - (_____)
	C - (_____)
Punch: _____	R - (_____)
	Same C - (_____)
Tag: _____	New R - (_____)

Setup: _____	TA - (_____)
	C - (_____)
Punch: _____	R - (_____)
	Same C - (_____)
Tag: _____	New R - (_____)

• **Technique 2: Tag a Different Setup Target Assumption and Connector**

It's Your Turn!

In the same sample jokes below, notice each has a New TA - target assumption and New C - connector in the parentheses.

Next, recognize or invent a different meaning of the New C - connector and that will be your New R - reinterpretation.

Then write a tag for each joke that based on your New R - reinterpretation that shatters the New TA - target assumptions.

Setup: *"For Father's Day I took my father out."*   New TA - (biological dad)

New C - (father)

Punch: *"With a pair of scissors."*

Tag: New R - (   )

Answer on page 57

Setup: *"I play in a three piece band."*   New TA - (play instruments)

New C - (what they play)

Punch: *"We wear a three piece suit."*

Tag: New R - (   )

Answer on page 57

Continue Your Turn!

On the forms below, write in the same one-liner setups and punches you used on page 32.

Next, identify a different, New TA - target assumption and a New C - connector for each setup.

Then, for the New C - connector, recognize or invent a New R - reinterpretation.

Based on the New R – reinterpretation, write a tag for each joke that shatters the New TA - target assumption.

Setup: _____ New TA - (_____)

New C - (_____)

Punch: _____

Tag: _____ New R - (_____)

Setup: _____ New TA - (_____)

New C - (_____)

Punch: _____

Tag: _____ New R - (_____)

• Technique 3: Tag Based a New Target Assumption Created By the Punch

It's Your Turn!

For the same sample jokes below, first notice the TA - target assumption, C - connector, and R - reinterpretation to understand the structure of these jokes.

Next, recognize a New TA - target assumption created by the punch. Then ask, "What in the punch caused me to make that New TA - target assumption?" The answer will be your New C - connector (one thing with two meanings).

Then, identify or invent another meaning for the C- connector, this different meaning will be your New R - reinterpretation.

Finally, based on the New R - reinterpretation write a tag for the punch that makes your New TA - target assumption wrong.

Setup: *"For Father's Day, I took my father out."*	TA - (to dinner)
	C - (took out)
Punch: *"It only took seven shots."*	R - (to kill)
	New TA - (killed him)
	New C - (shots)
Tag:	New R - ( )

Answer on page 57

Setup: *"I play in a three piece band."*	TA - (three musicians)
	C - (three piece)
Punch: *"We wear a three piece suit."*	R - (three suits)
	New TA - (each has his own suit)
	New C - (wear a)
Tag:	New R - ( )

Answer on page 57

Continue Your Turn!

On the forms below, write in the same one-liner setups and punches you used on 32 or choose two different one-liner jokes. Then recognize the TA - target assumption, C - connector, and R - reinterpretation to understand their structure.

Based on the punch, identify a New TA – target assumption. Then ask, "What in the punch caused me to make that New TA - target assumption?" The answer will be your New C - connector.

Then, recognize or invent another meaning for the C- connector. This different meaning will be your New R - reinterpretation.

Finally, based on the New R - reinterpretation write a tag for the punch that makes your New TA - target assumption wrong.

Setup: _____   TA - (_____)

                                    C - (_____)

Punch: _____   R - (_____)

                                    New TA - (_____)

                                    New C - (_____)

Tag: _____   New R - (_____)

Setup: _____   TA - (_____)

                                    C - (_____)

Punch: _____   R - (_____)

                                    New TA - (_____)

                                    New C - (_____)

Tag: _____   New R - (_____)

Routine Builder

The Routine Builder is a process to help you assemble your jokes into a routine. Different people can take the same jokes and end up forming very different routines, so the Routine Builder is designed to allow for personal preference. There's nothing worse than wanting to do something your way while thinking you're supposed to do it another way. So always feel free to customize the Routine Builder and experiment until you find your own style of arranging jokes into a bit.

Here we go:

1. PUT EACH JOKE ON SEPARATE LINE

Put each joke on a separate line. If the joke has an indelibly linked tag or tags, you can place them all in the same paragraph because their order is already set. This will force you to look at all your jokes so you'll be familiar with them while considering how to put them into an order.

It's Your Turn!

Select a series of your own jokes on the same topic and form them into a routine by following the steps of the Routine Builder.

On the lines below and on page 38, write out each joke on a separate line. If the joke has an indelibly linked tag or tags, you can place them all in the same paragraph because their order is already set.

On the lines below and on page 38, write out all the jokes you want to turn into a routine.

Topic: _____

Jokes: _____

_____

_____

_____

_____

2. ORGANIZE THE JOKES INTO CATEGORIES

Evaluate your jokes and look for recurring ideas so you can place them into like groupings. Sometimes a joke from one premise will fit better with jokes from another premise. Some jokes will fit more than one category; make your best guess for now, you can always change it later. If you have a joke or two that doesn't fit any of your chosen categories, then put them at the end as miscellaneous.

It's Your Turn!

Write your jokes from pages 37 and 38 onto the forms below and page 40 in order to arrange them into similar categories. You can always rearrange them later.

Category: _____

Jokes: _____

_____

_____

_____

_____

_____

_____

Category: _____

Jokes: _____

_____

_____

_____

_____

_____

Category: _____

Jokes: _____

_____

_____

_____

_____

_____

_____

Category: _____

Jokes: _____

_____

_____

_____

_____

Miscellaneous: _____

_____

_____

_____

_____

3. ARRANGE JOKES SO ONE THOUGHT LEADS TO THE NEXT

With your jokes sorted into categories, it's time to arrange the pieces of this puzzle into a connected series of thoughts. It should express *your* funny thoughts about the topic.

It's Your Turn!

On the lines below, decided on an order for your categories.

Category 1: _____

Category 2: _____

Category 3: _____

Category 4: _____

Continue Your Turn!

Using the forms on pages 42 and 43, write out your jokes according to the order of your categories so one thought leads to the next. This will be your first draft, so you can always change or rearrange things later.

Topic: _____

Routine: _____

_____

_____

_____

_____

_____

_____

_____

_____

_____

_____

_____

_____

_____

_____

_____

_____

_____

_____

Routine: _____

_____

_____

_____

_____

_____

_____

_____

_____

_____

_____

_____

_____

_____

_____

_____

_____

_____

_____

4. REWRITE, REWRITE, REWRITE

You'll need to experiment with wording, editing and reordering to make the jokes flow as a routine. When you're rewriting - *read the jokes out loud*. You'll quickly discover if it's awkward to bring up your topic, how clunky it is to go from one category to the next, where you've overwritten and when things sound artificial.

Refer to **Workbook 1: How to Write Jokes** in the section the **Joke Map** to understand the terms topic, punch-premise and setup-premise used in this section.

Introduce the Routine

It's so unnatural to just come on stage and start saying your first joke. You'll want to bring up the subject matter of your routine in the same way that you'd bring it up in normal conversation. You can do this in three ways:

• State the Topic

The purpose is to bring up your subject matter in a conversational manner in a way that doesn't draw attention to the fact that you changing subjects. If you use this approach, keep it simple.

Topic: Post office _____

State the Topic: "How can I bring up the subject of the post office without _____

sounding angry? I can't." _____

It's Your Turn!

On the forms below write several introductions where you state the topic of your routine.

Topic: _____

State the Topic: _____

_____

Topic: _____

State the Topic: _____

_____

• Proclaim the Punch-Premise

Sometimes stating the topic isn't enough because the routine requires more information for it to make sense. Proclaiming your punch-premise includes its negative opinion and may need additional information to frame the routine. Just copying the punch-premise from the Joke Prospector probably won't suffice; you'll have to write it as a regular thought.

Here's an example:

Topic: Post office

Punch-Premise: Postal workers are incompetent

Punch-Premise Introduction: *"I had to go to the post office the other day it's amazing how incompetent they are. For instance..."*

It's Your Turn!

On the forms below write several introductions using the subject and negative opinion from your punch-premises.

Topic:

Punch-Premise:

Punch-Premise Introduction:

Topic:

Punch-Premise:

Punch-Premise Introduction:

• Present the Setup-Premise

Some routines will have more of an impact by presenting the setup-premise's positive opinion, which will often be performed as sarcasm. Word your setup-premise conversationally, rather than transcribing it from the Joke Map.

Here's an example:

Topic: Post office

Setup-Premise: Postal workers are competent

Setup-Premise Introduction: *"Love going to the post office. The place is a testament to efficiency and competence."*

It's Your Turn!

On the forms below write several introductions using the subject and positive opinion from your setup-premises.

Topic:

Setup-Premise:

Setup-Premise Introduction:

Topic:

Setup-Premise:

Setup-Premise Introduction:

Add Segues

Segues are transitions between routines, premises or jokes. Many comedians find segues to be a waste of time. They're old-fashioned and harbor many of the hacky comics' clichés. The best segue is when the comedian just thinks about what's next and the audience automatically anticipates a change in subject. When a routine or bit is just too clumsy without a segue, by all means write one in, but do so sparingly.

Here's an example:

Last Joke of Bit: "I bought an autographed picture of Jesus."

Segue: "Hey, but it wasn't all bad."

First Joke of New Bit: "I also found a store that was having a pre-fire sale."

It's Your Turn!

On the form below, write the last joke of a bit and the first joke of a new bit for which you need a transition. Then write a segue that closes the gap between the two different subjects.

Last Joke of Bit:

Segue:

First Joke of New Bit:

Last Joke of Bit:

Segue:

First Joke of New Bit:

Search for a Story Line

At this point, what you have are clusters of jokes in categories. As you read the jokes out loud and play with the order, notice if there's a pattern within all this material to support a small story line. Its purpose is to help you move logically from one category to the next. It can be as simple as going somewhere or doing something.

Here's an example:

Category: Post office line _____

Category: Rude postal workers _____

Category: Buying stamps _____

Story Line: I go to the post office for some stamps and deal with standing

in a long line and rude postal workers. _____

It's Your Turn!

Look over all the categories and search for a thorough line that will support the entire routine. Then on the form below and page 54 write your story line.

Category: _____

Category: _____

Category: _____

Category: _____

Category: _____

Category: _____

Story Line: _____

_____

Category: _____

Category: _____

Category: _____

Category: _____

Category: _____

Category: _____

Story Line: _____

_____

Category: _____

Category: _____

Category: _____

Category: _____

Category: _____

Category: _____

Story Line: _____

_____

WRITE A ROUTINE

Based on all this advice, write an introduction which includes the topic or premise with its subject and negative opinion along with the story line. Then order your categories so they flow from one thought to the next along the story line. This arrangement is the first draft of the routine. Rewrite, reorder or change anything so it feels like your normal conversation.

It's Your Turn!

On the lines below, and on pages 56 and 57, jot down your topic, write an introduction and then arrange your categories along the story line to express your funny thoughts to create a routine.

Topic: _____

Punch-Premise: _____

Introduction: _____

_____

_____

Routine: _____

_____

_____

_____

_____

_____

_____

_____

Routine Cont'd: _____

_____

_____

_____

_____

_____

_____

_____

_____

_____

_____

_____

_____

_____

_____

_____

_____

_____

_____

<u>Routine Cont'd:</u> _____

_____

_____

_____

_____

_____

_____

_____

_____

_____

_____

_____

_____

_____

_____

_____

_____

_____

Answers to Exercises

ECONOMY

Joke: *"Postal workers put in hours of overtime. They leave the post office and go to a bar and drink for hours."*

Rewrite: *"Postal workers put in hours of overtime... at the bar."*
Answer for page 2

END THE PUNCH WITH THE REVEAL

• *Unnecessary words are said or actions are done after the reveal*

Joke: *"He has a contagious smile. Chlamydia or some other disgusting oral disease."*

Rewrite: "He has a contagious smile. Chlamydia."
Answer for page 4

• *The reveal gets mixed up with other important information*

Joke: *"After just four karate lessons, I could use my cast to break a two inch board."*

Rewrite: *"After just four karate lessons, I could break a two inch board with my cast."*
Answer for page 6

Answers to Exercises

USE WORDS OR PHRASES WITH HARD CONSONANTS

Joke: *"I hate singles bars. Guys come up to me and say, 'Hey, sweetie, can I buy you a drink?' I say, 'No, but I'll take the three dollars.'"*

Rewrite: *"I hate singles bars. Guys come up to me and say, 'Hey, cupcake, can I buy you a drink?' I say, 'No, but I'll take the three bucks.'"*

Answer for page 8

USE RHYTHMS OF THREE

Joke with List: *"I can persuade any woman to sleep with me just with flowers, chocolates and some romantic music."*

Rewrite with Rhythm of Three: *"I can persuade any woman to sleep with me just with flowers, romantic music, and some duct tape."*

Answer for page 10

STICK TO THE COMMON REALM OF KNOWLEDGE

Joke: *"I think Vlad the Impailer would have enjoyed watching the Three Stooges."*

Rewrite: *"I think the Marquis de Sade would have enjoyed watching the Three Stooges."*

Answer for page 12

Answers to Exercises

WRITE DIALOGUE WHENEVER POSSIBLE

Narrator Joke: *"After he lost the World Series of Poker, he said he slept like a baby. All night long, he'd sleep for an hour, then cry for an hour."*

Rewrite with Dialogue: (Commentator) *"After you lost the World Series of Poker, how did you deal with it?"* (Poker Player) *"I slept like a baby. All night long, I'd sleep for an hour, then cry for an hour."*

Answer for page 13

REGIONALIZE YOUR REFERENCES

Joke: *"Postal workers put in hours of overtime... at the bar."*

Regionalize: *"Postal workers put in hours of overtime... at Hooters."*

Answer for page 21

USING GRAMMATICALLY INCORRECT LANGUAGE IS OKAY

Formal Language: *"A guy from the Louisiana swamp told me they have mosquitoes so large that they have ticks."*

Common Language: *"A guy from Louziana told me, 'In dis here swamp, we done got skeeters so big dat day got ticks.'"*

Answer for page 24

Answers to Exercises

SOMETIMES A SIGHT GAG IS BETTER

Verbal Joke: *"All my girlfriend wanted for Valentine's Day was a card...*

American Express Platinum."

Sight Gag: (Take an American Express Platinum card out of your wallet and

show it to the audience.)

Answer for page 29

TAG YOUR JOKES

• Technique 1: Tag the Same Target Assumption and Connector, Again

Setup: *"For Father's Day I took my father out."*

Punch: *"With a pair of scissors."*

Tag: *"I cut him right out of the family photos."*

Answers for page 31

Or any idea with a different meaning of the connector "took out."

Setup: *"I play in a three piece band."*

Punch: *"We wear a three piece suit."*

Tag: *"And we only play three pieces."*

Answers for page 32

Or any idea with a different meaning of the connector "three piece."

Answers to Exercises

• **Technique 2: Tag a Different Setup Target Assumption and Connector**

Setup: *"For Father's Day I took my father out."*   (man who raised you)

Punch: *"It only took seven shots."*

Tag: *"I couldn't stand the way he did mass."*   (priest)

Answers for page 33
Or any idea with a different meaning of "father."

Setup: *"I play in a three piece band."*   (play instruments)

Punch: *"We wear a three piece suit."*

Tag: *"It's hard to play a suit."*   (play the suit)

Answers for page 33
Or any idea with a different meaning of "what is played."

• **Technique 3: Tag Based a New Target Assumption Created By the Punch**

Setup: *"For Father's Day, I took my father out."*

Punch: *"It only took seven shots."*   (seven drinks)

Tag: *"I drank him under the table."*

Answers for page 35
Or any idea based on an assumption from the punch.

Setup: *"I play in a three piece band."*

Punch: *"We wear a three piece suit."*   (each has their own suit)

Tag: *"The same suit."*

Answers for page 35
Or any idea based on an assumption from the punch.

What's Next?

Congratulations! You've finished *Workbook 2: How to Improve Jokes and Routines*, therefore you know how to make your jokes funnier and turn them into routines. So, here's the next step in the Greg Dean's Step By Step to Stand-Up Comedy – Workbook Series:

Workbook 3: How to Remember Jokes Naturally teaches you how to stage a comedy act-out or scene as well as rehearse your routines without memorizing the words so you can tell funny stories just as you do in everyday life.

Step By Step to Stand-Up Comedy – Workbook Series
Available at stand-upcomedy.com. Get all five...I'll be glad you did.

✓ **Workbook 1: How to Write Jokes**

Learn and practice the skills of joke writing with Greg Dean's system the *Joke Prospector*. Never written a joke? By the end of this workbook you will.

✓ **Workbook 2: How to Improve Jokes and Routines**

Now that you have jokes, learn the techniques of taking your already funny jokes and making them even funnier and then arrange them into a comedy routine.

Workbook 3: How to Remember Jokes Naturally

With your jokes formed into routines, learn to remember your jokes as if you're telling a story without memorizing the words.

Workbook 4: How to Be a Funny Performer

Before getting on stage, learn all the tricks of the trade only professional comedians know. These performing techniques will make you look polished.

Workbook 5: How to Get the Experience to Be Funny

Now you are ready to perform. Only stage time will help you learn how to apply all the techniques and skills you've learn in this workbook series. Enjoy.

Greg Dean's Comedy Store

Step By Step to Stand-Up Comedy

- **Step By Step to Stand-Up Comedy – Paperback**
  Don't already have this book? You're missing out on the best book written for beginner comedians. It's the book on which this workbook series is based.
  Order Now @ stand-upcomedy.com

- **Step By Step to Stand-Up Comedy – eBook**
  You can read the original book on a smart phone, iPad, Kindle, or Nook anytime, anywhere. Order Now @ stand-upcomedy.com

- **Step By Step to Stand-Up Comedy – Audio Book**
  Too busy to read, now you can listen to the original book read by the author Greg Dean. Order Now @ stand-upcomedy.com

Inside the Stand-Up Studio - DVD
  Learn the fundamentals of how to be a stand-up comedian with Greg Dean. Dean demonstrates joke writing, act outs, microphone technique, rehearsal and performing. This is the whole package in one DVD.
  Order Now @ stand-upcomedy.com

From Funny to Funnier:
Extra Forms

ECONOMY

Joke: _____

_____

Rewrite: _____

_____

Joke: _____

_____

Rewrite: _____

_____

Joke: _____

_____

Rewrite: _____

_____

Joke: _____

_____

Rewrite: _____

_____

END THE PUNCH WITH THE REVEAL

• **Unnecessary words are said or actions are done after the reveal**

Joke: _____

_____

Rewrite: _____

_____

_____

Joke: _____

_____

Rewrite: _____

_____

_____

Joke: _____

_____

Rewrite: _____

_____

_____

Joke: _____

_____

Rewrite: _____

_____

_____

• The reveal gets mixed up with other important information

Joke: _____

_____

Rewrite: _____

_____

_____

Joke: _____

_____

Rewrite: _____

_____

_____

Joke: _____

_____

Rewrite: _____

_____

_____

Joke: _____

_____

Rewrite: _____

_____

_____

USE WORDS OR PHRASES WITH HARD CONSONANTS

Joke: _____

_____

Rewrite: _____

_____

_____

Joke: _____

_____

Rewrite: _____

_____

_____

Joke: _____

_____

Rewrite: _____

_____

_____

Joke: _____

_____

Rewrite: _____

_____

_____

USE RHYTHMS OF THREE

Joke with List: _____

_____

Rewrite with Rhythm of Three: _____

_____

_____

Joke with List: _____

_____

Rewrite with Rhythm of Three: _____

_____

_____

Joke with List: _____

_____

Rewrite with Rhythm of Three: _____

_____

_____

STICK TO THE COMMON REALM OF KNOWLEDGE

Joke: _____

_____

Rewrite: _____

_____

_____

Joke: _____

_____

Rewrite: _____

_____

_____

Joke: _____

_____

Rewrite: _____

_____

_____

Joke: _____

_____

Rewrite: _____

_____

_____

WRITE DIALOGUE WHENEVER POSSIBLE

Narrator Joke: _____

_____

Rewrite with Dialogue: _____

_____

_____

Narrator Joke: _____

_____

Rewrite with Dialogue: _____

_____

_____

Narrator Joke: _____

_____

Rewrite with Dialogue: _____

_____

_____

MAKE YOUR CHARACTERS SPECIFIC AND REAL

CHARACTER PROFILE FORM #1

Joke: _____

_____

_____

Name: _____

Job: _____

Sex: _____

Age: _____

Height: _____

Weight _____

National Heritage: _____

Voice: _____

Posture: _____

Walk: _____

Characteristics or Taints: _____

General Attitude: _____

Idiosyncrasies: _____

Agenda: _____

Religion: _____

Notes after Being the Character: _____

_____

_____

_____

_____

Rewrite the Joke: _____

_____

_____

_____

MAKE YOUR CHARACTERS SPECIFIC AND REAL

CHARACTER PROFILE FORM #2

Joke: _____

_____

_____

Name: _____

Job: _____

Sex: _____

Age: _____

Height: _____

Weight: _____

National Heritage: _____

Voice: _____

Posture: _____

Walk: _____

Characteristics or Taints: _____

General Attitude: _____

Idiosyncrasies: _____

Agenda: _____

Religion: _____

<u>Notes after Being the Character:</u>

_____

_____

_____

_____

<u>Rewrite the Joke:</u>

_____

_____

_____

REGIONALIZE YOUR REFERENCES

Joke: _____

_____

Regionalize: _____

_____

_____

Joke: _____

_____

Regionalize: _____

_____

_____

Joke: _____

_____

Regionalize: _____

_____

_____

Joke: _____

_____

Regionalize: _____

_____

_____

CALENDAR DAY JOKES

Calendar Day: _____

Joke or Bit: _____

_____

_____

Calendar Day: _____

Joke or Bit: _____

_____

_____

Calendar Day: _____

Joke or Bit: _____

_____

_____

Calendar Day: _____

Joke or Bit: _____

_____

_____

USING GRAMMATICALLY INCORRECT LANGUAGE IS OKAY

Formal Language: _____

_____

Common Language: _____

_____

Formal Language: _____

_____

Common Language: _____

_____

Formal Language: _____

_____

Common Language: _____

_____

Formal Language: _____

_____

Common Language: _____

_____

SOMETIMES A SIGHT GAG IS BETTER

Verbal Joke: _____

_____

Sight Gag: _____

_____

Verbal Joke: _____

_____

Sight Gag: _____

_____

Verbal Joke: _____

_____

Sight Gag: _____

_____

Verbal Joke: _____

_____

Sight Gag: _____

_____

TAG YOUR JOKES

• **Technique 1: Tag the Same Target Assumption and Connector, Again**

Setup: _____ TA - (   )
                                         C - (   )
Punch: _____ R - (   )

                                      Same C - (   )

Tag: _____ New R - (   )

Setup: _____ TA - (   )
                                         C - (   )
Punch: _____ R - (   )

                                      Same C - (   )

Tag: _____ New R - (   )

Setup: _____ TA - (   )
                                         C - (   )
Punch: _____ R - (   )

                                      Same C - (   )

Tag: _____ New R - (   )

Setup: _____ TA - (   )
                                         C - (   )
Punch: _____ R - (   )

                                      Same C - (   )

Tag: _____ New R - (   )

TAG YOUR JOKES

• Technique 2: Tag a Different Setup Target Assumption and Connector

Setup: _____   New TA - (_____)

Punch: _____   New C - (_____)

Tag: _____   New R - (_____)

Setup: _____   New TA - (_____)

Punch: _____   New C - (_____)

Tag: _____   New R - (_____)

Setup: _____   New TA - (_____)

Punch: _____   New C - (_____)

Tag: _____   New R - (_____)

Setup: _____   New TA - (_____)

Punch: _____   New C - (_____)

Tag: _____   New R - (_____)

TAG YOUR JOKES

• Technique 3: Tag Based a New Target Assumption Created By the Punch

Setup: _____ TA - (_____)

C - (_____)

Punch: _____ R - (_____)

New TA - (_____)

New C - (_____)

Tag: _____ New R - (_____)

Setup: _____ TA - (_____)

C - (_____)

Punch: _____ R - (_____)

New TA - (_____)

New C - (_____)

Tag: _____ New R - (_____)

Setup: _____ TA - (_____)

C - (_____)

Punch: _____ R - (_____)

New TA - (_____)

New C - (_____)

Tag: _____ New R - (_____)

Setup: _____ TA - (_____)

C - (_____)

Punch: _____ R - (_____)

New TA - (_____)

New C - (_____)

Tag: _____ New R - (_____)

Routine Builder:
Extra Forms #1

1. PUT EACH JOKE ON SEPARATE LINE

Topic: _____

Jokes: _____

_____

_____

_____

_____

_____

_____

_____

_____

_____

_____

_____

_____

_____

_____

_____

2. ORGANIZE THE JOKES INTO CATEGORIES

Category: _____

Jokes: _____

_____

_____

_____

_____

_____

_____

Category: _____

Jokes: _____

_____

_____

_____

_____

_____

Category: _____

Jokes: _____

_____

_____

_____

_____

_____

_____

Category: _____

Jokes: _____

_____

_____

_____

_____

_____

_____

Miscellaneous: _____

_____

_____

_____

3. ARRANGE JOKES SO ONE THOUGHT LEADS TO THE NEXT

Category 1: _____

Category 2: _____

Category 3: _____

 Category 4: _____

Topic: _____

Routine: _____

_____

_____

_____

_____

_____

_____

_____

_____

_____

_____

_____

_____

_____

3. ARRANGE JOKES SO ONE THOUGHT LEADS TO THE NEXT

Routine: _____

_____

_____

_____

_____

_____

_____

_____

_____

_____

_____

_____

_____

_____

_____

_____

_____

_____

4. REWRITE, REWRITE, REWRITE

Introduce the Routine

• State the Topic

Topic: _____

State the Topic: _____

_____

Topic: _____

State the Topic: _____

_____

• Proclaim the Punch-Premise

Topic: _____

Punch-Premise: _____

Punch-Premise Introduction: _____

_____

Topic: _____

Punch-Premise: _____

Punch-Premise Introduction: _____

_____

• Present the Setup-Premise

Topic: _____

Setup-Premise: _____

Setup-Premise Introduction: _____

_____

Topic: _____

Setup-Premise: _____

Setup-Premise Introduction: _____

_____

Add Segues

Last Joke of Bit: _____

_____

Segue: _____

First Joke of New Bit: _____

_____

Last Joke of Bit: _____

_____

Segue: _____

First Joke of New Bit: _____

_____

Search for a Story Line

Category: _____

Category: _____

Category: _____

Category: _____

Category: _____

Story Line: _____

_____

Category: _____

Category: _____

Category: _____

Category: _____

Category: _____

Story Line: _____

_____

WRITE A ROUTINE

Topic: _____

Punch-Premise: _____

Introduction: _____

_____

_____

Routine: _____

_____

_____

_____

_____

_____

_____

_____

_____

_____

_____

_____

_____

_____

_____

Routine Cont'd: _____

_____

_____

_____

_____

_____

_____

_____

_____

_____

_____

_____

_____

_____

_____

_____

_____

Routine Cont'd:

Routine Builder:
Extra Forms #2

1. PUT EACH JOKE ON SEPARATE LINE

Topic: _____

Jokes: _____

_____

_____

_____

_____

_____

_____

_____

_____

_____

_____

_____

_____

_____

_____

2. ORGANIZE THE JOKES INTO CATEGORIES

Category: _____

Jokes: _____

_____

_____

_____

_____

_____

_____

Category: _____

Jokes: _____

_____

_____

_____

_____

_____

_____

Category: _____

Jokes: _____

_____

_____

_____

_____

_____

Category: _____

Jokes: _____

_____

_____

_____

_____

_____

Miscellaneous: _____

_____

_____

_____

3. ARRANGE JOKES SO ONE THOUGHT LEADS TO THE NEXT

Category 1: _____

Category 2: _____

Category 3: _____

 Category 4: _____

Topic: _____

Routine: _____

_____

_____

_____

_____

_____

_____

_____

_____

_____

_____

_____

_____

Routine: _____

_____

_____

_____

_____

_____

_____

_____

_____

_____

_____

_____

_____

_____

_____

_____

_____

_____

_____

4. REWRITE, REWRITE, REWRITE

Introduce the Routine

• State the Topic

    Topic: _____

    State the Topic: _____

    _____

    Topic: _____

    State the Topic: _____

    _____

• Proclaim the Punch-Premise

    Topic: _____

    Punch-Premise: _____

    Punch-Premise Introduction: _____

    _____

    Topic: _____

    Punch-Premise: _____

    Punch-Premise Introduction: _____

    _____

• Present the Setup-Premise

Topic: _____

Setup-Premise: _____

Setup-Premise Introduction: _____

_____

Topic: _____

Setup-Premise: _____

Setup-Premise Introduction: _____

_____

Add Segues

Last Joke of Bit: _____

_____

Segue: _____

First Joke of New Bit: _____

_____

Last Joke of Bit: _____

_____

Segue: _____

First Joke of New Bit: _____

_____

Search for a Story Line

Category: _____

Category: _____

Category: _____

Category: _____

Category: _____

Story Line: _____

_____

Category: _____

Category: _____

Category: _____

Category: _____

Category: _____

Story Line: _____

_____

WRITE A ROUTINE

Topic: _____

Punch-Premise: _____

Introduction: _____

_____

_____

Routine: _____

_____

_____

_____

_____

_____

_____

_____

_____

_____

_____

_____

_____

_____

Routine Cont'd: _____

_____

_____

_____

_____

_____

_____

_____

_____

_____

_____

_____

_____

_____

_____

_____

_____